LET'S
see

Voting and Elections

by Patricia J. Murphy

Content Adviser: Professor Sherry L. Field, Department of Social Science Education,

College of Education, The University of Georgia

Reading Adviser: Dr. Linda D. Labbo, Department of Reading Education,

College of Education, The University of Georgia

Let's See Library

Compass Point Books

Minneapolis, Minnesota

Compass Point Books
1710 Roe Crest Drive
North Mankato, MN 56003
877-845-8392
www.capstonepub.com

 This book was manufactured with paper containing
at least 10 percent post-consumer waste.

Photographs ©: Pictor/Charles Gupton, cover, 6; Reuters/Barbara Johnston/Archive Photos, 4; Reuters/Rick
Wilking/Archive Photos, 8; Bettmann/Corbis, 10; Pictor/Bill Auth, 12; Victor Malafronte/Archive Photos,
14; Pictor/Bob Daemmrich, 16; Stock Montage, 18; Reuters NewMedia, Inc./Corbis, 20.

Editors: E. Russell Primm and Emily J. Dolbear
Photo Researcher: Svetlana Zhurkina
Photo Selector: Phyllis Rosenberg
Designer: Melissa Voda

Library of Congress Cataloging-in-Publication Data
Murphy, Patricia J., 1963–
    Voting and elections / by Patricia J. Murphy.
      p. cm. — (Let's see library. Our nation)
    Includes bibliographical references (p.) and index.
    ISBN 978-0-7565-0144-0 (library binding)
    ISBN 978-0-7565-1471-6 (paperback)
    1. Elections—United States—Juvenile literature. 2. Voting—United States—Juvenile literature. [1.
Elections. 2. Voting.] I. Title. II. Series.
    JK1978 .M87 2002
    324.6'0973—dc21   2001001586

Printed in the United States of America in North Mankato, Minnesota.
102012   006969

Table of Contents

What Is Voting?

Voting is a way of choosing someone or something. The people of the United States choose their leaders by voting. Some leaders run towns, cities, and states. Other leaders run the country.

Sometimes people **vote** for projects that will help their city or town. They also vote against projects that may hurt their city or town. For example, if the people of a town vote "yes," the town will build a new road. If the people vote "no," the town will not build the new road.

◀ *Christine Whitman was the first female governor of New Jersey.*

How Do People Vote?

All the people vote on the same day. They go to special places to vote. These places are called **polls**.

Some polling places have special machines. People vote by pulling a lever on the machine. Other people vote by making a mark on a sheet of paper. These sheets of paper are called ballots. Sometimes people vote by punching a hole in the ballot.

◄ *Voting is done by marking a ballot.*

What Is an Election?

Voting for a leader is called an election. There are many kinds of elections. In some elections, people pick the mayor of their town or the governor of their state. In an election for president, people pick the leader of their country. In the United States, an election to choose a president is held every four years.

◄ *President George W. Bush (left) and Vice President Richard Cheney were elected in 2000.*

What Is a Candidate?

A person who wants to be chosen to be a leader is called a **candidate**. Many candidates may want the job. They all hope to make good things happen in their town, state, or country. They all promise to work hard. In an election, people can vote for only one candidate for each office. The candidate who gets the most votes wins the election.

◄ *In 1960, John F. Kennedy traveled through California meeting voters.*

What Is a Political Party?

A political party is a group of people who share ideas on many subjects. They agree on what makes a good leader. They also agree on the best way to run their city, state, or country.

There are two main political parties in the United States. They are the Democratic Party and the Republican Party. Most candidates belong to one of these parties. Most voters belong to one of these parties too.

◄ *Bill Clinton and Al Gore were the candidates chosen at the Democratic National Convention in 1992. They ran for president and vice president.*

Who Is Elected?

The people of the United States **elect** the president and the vice president of the country. They also choose the people who make the laws. The people who make the laws are called senators and representatives. They work in Congress.

The people of each state choose their own state leaders. They elect the governor. They also elect the people who make state laws.

The people of each town and city choose their own leaders too. They elect the mayor, sheriff, and other leaders.

◄ *The people of New York chose George Pataki to be their governor in 1994 and 1998.*

INFORMACION GENERAL PARA VOTANTES

...do desee. Para poder inscribirse, debe haber cumplido no menos de 17 años con 10 meses. Su
...te en la fecha que ocurra mas tarde, que sea: a los 30 días de su recibo o al cumplir usted los 18 años.
...ANO/A DE LOS ESTADOS UNIDOS PARA INSCRIBIRSE. En caso de haberse cambiado a otro
...en su nuevo condado de residencia.

...ara votar, su negativa a inscribirse se mantendrá confidencial y sólo será utilizada para fines del registro electoral.
...se inscribe para votar se mantendrá confidencial la identidad de la oficina (si la hay) en que presentó su solicitud de
...otar. Esta información sólo será utilizada para fines del registro electoral.

* Separe la parte de abajo siguiendo la línea de puntos y devuélvala al Registrador de Votantes.

VOTER REGISTRATION APPLICATION
(SOLICITUD DE INSCRIPCION DE VOTANTE)

...by the
...ary of State
17.95 BPM1.1-96

For Official Use Only
PCT   Cert. Num.
EDR

Last Name (Apellido usual)	First Name (NOT HUSBAND'S) Su nombre de pila (Siendo mujer: no el del esposo)	Middle Name (If any) (Segundo Nombre) (si tiene)	Former Name (Nombre anterior)
Flowers	Melanie	Leslie	

Residence Address: Street Address and Apartment Number, City, State, and ZIP. If none, describe where you live. (Do not include P.O. Box or Rural Rt.)
(Domicilio: Calle y número, número de apartamento, Ciudad, Estado, y Código Postal; A falta de estos datos, describa su localidad de su residencia.) (No incluya su apartado postal ni su ruta rural.)

225 Birch Lane, Austin TX 18756

Mailing Address, City, State and ZIP: If mail cannot be delivered to your residence address. (Dirección postal, Ciudad, Estado y
Código Postal) (Si es imposible entregarle correspondencia a domicilio.)

1050 Pecan Drive, Dallas, TX

Gender (Optional) (Sexo) (Optativo)
☒ Male (Hombre) ☐ Female (Mujer)

Date of Birth: month, day, year (Fecha de Nacimiento:) (mes, día, año)	City, County, and State of Former Residence (Ciudad, Condado, Estado de su residencia anterior)	Social Security No. (Optional) (Número de Seguro Social)(optativo)
10-9-77	Austin	389-50-1513

TX Driver's License No. or Personal I.D. No. (Issued by TX Dept. of Public Safety) (Optional) (Número de su licencia tejana de manejar o de su Cédula de Identidad expedida por el Departamento de Seguridad Pública de Tejas) (optativo)

Check appropriate box: I am a United States Citizen ☒ Yes (Sí) ☐ No (No)
(Marque el cuadro apropiado: Soy Ciudadano/a de los Estados Unidos)

I understand that giving false information to procure a voter registration is perjury, and a crime under state and federal law. (Entiendo que el hecho de proporcionar datos falsos a fin de obtener inscripción en el registro de votantes, constituye el delito de perjurio o declaración falsa y es una infracción sancionable por ley federal y estatal.)

Telephone Number (Optional) (Número telefónico) (optativo)

I affirm that I (Declaro que soy)
• **am a resident of this county;** (residente del condado)
• **have not been finally convicted of a felony or if a felon I am eligible for registration under section 13.001, Election Code; and**
(que no he sido condenado/a en definitiva por un delito penal, o en caso de tal condena, que estoy habilitado/a para inscribirme, a tenor de lo dispuesto por la sección 13.001 del Código Electoral)
• **have not been declared mentally incompetent by final judgment of a court of law.**
(no se me ha declarado mentalmente incapacitado por orden judicial.)

Date (fecha)

X _Melanie Flowers_

Signature of Applicant or Agent and Relationship to Applicant or Printed Name of Applicant if Signed by Witness and Date. (Firma debida la solicitant... su apoderado/a y qué parentesco tiene c/la apoderado/a con c/la solicitante. Si la firma es de testigo, escriba el nombre debida la solicitante usando letra de molde y ponga la fecha.)

Who Can Vote?

To vote in the United States, a person must be a **citizen** of the United States. A citizen is a person who was born in a certain place or has the right to live there. A voter must be at least eighteen years old.

Before people can vote, they must sign up, or register. People register to vote in a city or state office. After filling out a special form, they are given a voter's card. In some places, a person must show a voter's card before voting. Each person's name is also kept on a list of voters checked at the polling places.

◄ *You must fill out a voter's registration card application form before you can vote.*

When Can You Vote?

When you are eighteen years old, you will be able to vote. What year will you turn eighteen years old? On that birthday, remember to register to vote. You can play an important part in choosing the leaders of your town, state, and country.

Until then, you can vote in your classroom. You can also vote in clubs and with your friends. When the group has to make a big decision, ask everyone to vote! That way, everyone has a say.

◄ *People line up to vote.*

What Does Voting Mean to People?

Many people have fought hard for the right to vote. At one time, poor people in the United States could not vote. African-Americans and women could not vote either. Even now, people in many other countries still do not have the right to vote.

Voting is a special right. People who vote choose their own leaders. They help decide what happens to them. They also help make decisions that can help others too. People who vote help shape the world around them.

◀ *African-American men were first allowed to vote in 1870.*

Glossary

candidate—a person who wants to be chosen as a leader in an election

citizen—a person who is born in a country or has the right to live there

elect—to choose a person as a leader

polls—special places where people go to vote

vote—to choose someone or something

Did You Know?

• The election for president is always held on the first Tuesday after the first Monday of November. The election was first held in November so that the farmers would be able to vote once their work in the fields was done!

• Women in the United States did not have the right to vote until 1920.

Want to Know More?

More Books to Read

Heath, David. *Elections in the United States*. Mankato, Minn.: Capstone Press, 1999.

Henry, Christopher E. *Presidential Elections*. Danbury, Conn.: Franklin Watts, 1996.

Quiri, Patricia Ryon. *The Presidency*. Danbury, Conn.: Children's Press, 1998.

On the Web

For more information on this topic, use FactHound.

1. Go to *www.facthound.com*
2. Choose your grade level.
3. Begin your search.

This book's ID number is 9780756501440.

FactHound will find the best sites for you.

Through the Mail

Kids Voting USA

398 South Mill Avenue, Suite 304

Tempe, AZ 85281

To find out how you can visit a polling place on election day and fill out your own ballot

On the Road

U.S. Capitol

Washington DC 20515

202/225-6827

To visit the rooms where our elected senators and representatives make the laws of our country. The Capitol is open every day except New Year's Day, Thanksgiving, and Christmas.

Index

About the Author
Patricia J. Murphy has written many books for children including storybooks, nonfiction, early readers, and poetry. She received a bachelor's degree in journalism from Northern Illinois University and a master's degree from National Louis University. Ms. Murphy has taught in the Lake Forest public schools. She lives in Northbrook, Illinois.